Fatal Myth

by Henry H. Hamer

To Humankind

Amazon.com

Manufactured in the United
States of America

The Fatal Myth
(that memory is reliable)

There is a view that memory is reliable. Memories are not reliable. Nonetheless many people believe their memories are reliable, and in turn, rely on them even at the risk of life and limb. Regardless of the fact that the unreliability of the memory would be accepted by most people as an observable, though regrettable fact, most people still unconsciously go about their day confident of the accuracy of their memory. A strange default pattern in our thinking.

Hospitals, doctors and pharmacists would not think of operating on a basis of mere oral orders; orders must be written down. Memories even with the best of intentions can be faulty. Not only might the one giving the order fail to include a key element, but the one carrying out the order can drop out a similarly key element. Obviously even with written orders memory can lapse, and result in sudden and fatal errors when a drug is administered at the wrong dosage.

Similar memory slip ups can be seen through out the day. We remember our third grade teacher, or a thousand other people, things and events in our lives, and conclude our memory is still intact.

A number of published studies have proven just the opposite. A major example comes from today's criminal justice system and forensic science. Most of us are aware of the advances in the accuracy of evidence brought into the courtroom as a result of the study of DNA.   It has been determined that about 49% of prisoners currently serving time as a result of convictions based on eye witness testimony, were in fact wrongly convicted. Police and prosecutors are now less likely to rely solely on eye witness testimony. Memories are just not reliable.

And how susceptible is memory to outside manipulation, intentional or unintentional? Again using an example from criminal investigations: A detective might ask an eye witness who was the first to discover a dead body, "What color coat was the person wearing when you first saw him?" The question may have been an example of sloppy interrogation, or a deliberate attempt to suggest an element to the witness' memory. The witness might reply,

"Brown." Later in court it might be brought out that the body did not have a coat at all. This may be a rather innocuous example, but on the other hand we are all amazed at the frequency with which we hear of suspects worn down by long interrogations, confessing to crimes they did not commit. What was done to affect that person's memory? And how often are we complicit in this falsehood? We may shrug and say, "The police finally got it out of him. He probably did it." It wasn't someone we knew anyway. And we reaffirm that our memory is fine, and we would not confess to something we did not do. So again we default to trusting that memory is reliable.

Relationships can be severely damaged by assuming our memories are reliable and not altered by intentional or unintentional power of suggestion. Examples of this can include commitments to be at a certain place at a certain time or whether it be something important like picking up one's children. Memory lapses, failures or changes in memory are at the heart of the problem. It's also been shown that other people can influence our memories and can even change them for us. This forces us to look at some important questions that can affect our relationships, our well-being, and our happiness.

Have you ever had a miscommunication with your partner where both of you were adamant about what was said? In many cases, you may think your partner is not being honest because your memory is very clear to you.   Is it possible the memory of one or both of you changed? Or perhaps one of you heard incorrectly what the other said?   In a real-life example, a woman asked her husband if he "could turn off the light." However, he heard her say, "I am really turned onto you tonight."   Is it possible that his past memories allowed him to relate "lights off" with "sex?" In this case, his memories have caused a miscommunication. Can you see how he may feel rejected and let down after he gets into bed and his wife is not interested in him? A discussion the next morning could turn into an argument after confronting the wife and she does not recall telling her husband that she is turned on by him. Needless-to-say the husbands' ego has been hurt and the relationship may start to slip.

When we remember something, it may be slightly or totally different from what it was the last time we remembered it and, because we usually do not take time to create 'audit' trails (IE. Notes, pictures, etc.) to follow (IE: no coat, brown coat (later), gray coat (later still), etc. and, bring home milk, bread (later), juice (later still), etc., we may come home with chocolate milk, which no one wanted or wants now, but it is sort of brown, right? We may be so (unconsciously) guilty /

fearful / angry / defensive by that time and, after being or seeming to be attacked / betrayed / abandoned because of (possibly) overblown reactions, we may be feeling like storming out to the nearest bar, or worse, or much worse. Ever allow alcohol and sleepiness while driving to bring you close to killing someone in another vehicle, possibly a family, possibly yourself too?

Memory and

miscommunication issues don't just happen within spousal relationships of course. Are you concerned that the leaders of different countries are having similar issues? Could the language barrier be causing even more problems? Our safety may be indirectly or directly related to these issues.

Memory causing miscommunication could cause serious issues with any relationship you may have or any relationship you may be affected by, IE. teacher, parent, kids, government leaders, etc.

Miscommunication can affect what we thought we said or heard but have you considered that a memory that you have can be changed without your knowledge?

Are you comfortable that someone might change your memory of what you had for breakfast today?

Power of suggestion certainly changes memory as seen in the example with the witness believing the victim had a coat on. And there are other ways, again backed by scientific studies.

Most people have heard or seen instances where someone is forced into confession of a murder. It's hard to believe it could happen, but power of suggestion is very powerful.

Are you comfortable that thoughts can be planted into your head? This can happen intentionally or inadvertently.

We know today that energy work may transfer energy to another person. The energy worker may get a craving for say cool-aid while the client is thinking about cool-aid. Can these types of experiences mean that we can change another's memory? (Yes, and many scientific studies are in evidence.)

In what type of circumstance might someone try to change another's memory? And, how could that be done?

Do you ever experience a child manipulating a situation to get what they want? If a parent for example, is under stress and the child manipulates that she said he could go somewhere or give him money, the mother may believe she did say that. Is the child in this situation changing her memory?

Is it possible that written contracts are now common because "hand shakes" rely on memory.

Can you imagine the

situation where whatever another person says, you accept their memory unconditionally? This means entertaining the possibility that their memory is correct.

In the earlier example, if your partner says, I don't remember saying that I was attracted to you last night honey? Could that explanation be okay even though *your* memory says something else? Can you see how your feelings can escalate to feelings of rejection or abandonment if you weren't practicing unconditional love?

What if you were to change your *attachment* of your memories? Would your relationships be better?

If we want to improve the reliability of our memories, you may consider removing the attachments and practicing unconditional love.

Unconditional love means accepting what people say and do. It does not necessarily mean endorsing the actions of another person, or getting involved in it.

www.ingramcontent.com/pod-product-compliance
Lightning Source LLC
Chambersburg PA
CBHW070255290526
45789CB00004B/1866